W9-AZV-250

DATE DUE

06-7

320.97   Smalley, Carol Parenzan.
Sma   State and local government

EDMOND H. TAVEIRNE
MIDDLE SCHOOL
LEARNING CENTER
34699 N. Highway 12
Ingleside, IL 60041

WITHDRAWN

Reading Essentials®
in Social Studies

U.S. GOVERNMENT

State and Local Government

Carol Parenzan Smalley

PERFECTION LEARNING®

EDMOND H. TAVEIRNE
MIDDLE SCHOOL
LEARNING CENTER
34699 N. Highway 12
Ingleside, IL 60041

3000300030 0486

P.T.O.

06 - 7   # 18.95

EDITORIAL DIRECTOR	Susan C. Thies
EDITOR	Lucy Miller
EDITORIAL ASSISTANT	Kate Winzenburg
DESIGN DIRECTOR	Randy Messer
BOOK DESIGN	Emily J. Greazel
COVER DESIGN	Michael Aspengren

IMAGE CREDITS
© Associated Press: pp. 14, 15, 16 (top), 18, 20, 40; © Michael Appleton/CORBIS: p. 13;
© Bettmann/CORBIS: p. 16 (bottom); © Reuters/CORBIS: p. 37

ArtToday.com: p. 7; Bill Trojan/The Leader-Herald: p. 31; Corbis Royalty Free: front cover (small image),
back cover, pp. 29, 45, 46; Corel Professional Photos: front cover (small image), pp. 9 (bottom left), 39
(bottom); Image100: p. 21; Iowa Division of Tourism: p. 11; Library of Congress: p. 8; Liquid Library:
p. 43; Map Resources: p. 24; National Archives: p. 6; Perfection Learning: pp. 10, 32; PhotoDisc Royalty
Free: p. 28; Photos.com: front cover (small image), pp. 9 (top, bottom right), 12, 22, 23, 27, 30, 34, 38,
39 (top); South Dakota Department of Tourism: front cover (main image), p. 5; Tom Lorey: p. 26

Some images ClipArt.com, Iowa Division of Tourism, Library of Congress, Map Resources, PhotoDisc
Royalty Free, Photos.com: (Chapter heading bar) pp. 3, 4, 6, 11, 24, 36, 42–43

A special thanks to William J. Miller, attorney, for reviewing this book

Text © 2005 by **Perfection Learning® Corporation**.
All rights reserved. No part of this book may be reproduced, stored in
a retrieval system, or transmitted in any form or by any means,
electronic, mechanical, photocopying, recording,
or otherwise, without prior permission of the publisher.
Printed in the United States of America. For information, contact

Perfection Learning® Corporation
1000 North Second Avenue, P.O. Box 500
Logan, Iowa 51546-0500.
Tel: 1-800-831-4190 • Fax: 1-800-543-2745
perfectionlearning.com

1 2 3 4 5 6 PP 09 08 07 06 05 04

ISBN 0-7891-6245-8

Contents

State and Local Government at a Glance

General Facts

Number of State Governments   50

Longest State Constitution
  Alabama (approximately 220,000 words)

Shortest State Constitution
  Vermont (8,356 words)

Number of Counties
  3,066 (2004)

Number of Local Governments
  over 84,000

State with Fewest Counties/Parishes/Boroughs*
  Delaware (3 counties)
  *Louisiana does not have counties; it has **parishes**.
  Alaska does not have counties; it has **boroughs**.

State with Most Counties
  Texas (254)

Number of School Districts
  over 15,000

South Dakota's capitol building

A Multilevel Government System

Government in the United States is based on a multilevel system. The federal government has national powers. Individual states hold power within that state. And local governments preserve law and order on a community level. Each level has its own responsibilities, but they work together too.

The Articles of Confederation outlined the first type of national government that existed in this country. This document gave most of the governing powers to the states. But leaders throughout the country realized that if each state had its own powers, the new country would be weaker as a whole. The Founders decided to base their new country's government on **federalism**. Power would be shared between the federal government and individual states.

A multilevel government gives all people, as opposed to a select few, the power to control the government. It also offers many opportunities for citizens to be involved with the governing process.

The Articles of Confederation

Starting with Constitutions

The Constitution of the United States broadly outlines the responsibilities of national and state governments. It does not, however, explain the duties of local government. Each individual state has its own state constitution. The responsibilities of local government are often outlined in the state constitution.

Neither local laws nor state constitutions can contradict the U.S. Constitution, known as the Supreme Law of the Land.

The role of state government (and its associated local governments) has changed over the years. Important issues such as slavery and women's suffrage have brought about additions, or amendments, to the U.S. Constitution. These amendments limit power held by the state.

The 13th Amendment to the U.S. Constitution (ratified in 1865) made slavery illegal. Before this amendment, individual states decided the status of slavery within their own borders. With the ratification of the 13th Amendment, even states that believed in slavery had no choice but to follow the Constitution. When states refuse to **ratify** an amendment, they show that they disagree with the amendment. They still have to follow the law, however.

Slavery and the 13th Amendment

Here are some facts about slavery in various states.
★ Vermont was the first state to outlaw slavery in its constitution in 1777.
★ In Missouri, citizens debated in 1820 whether Missouri would enter the United States as a slave state or free state. Eventually, in what became known as the Missouri Compromise, Missouri entered as a slave state to balance Maine's entrance as a free state.
★ Kentucky was the last state to ratify the amendment, doing so in 1976.

The Nineteenth Amendment goes to the states.

Harriet Taylor Upton, Maud Wood Park, Mary Garrett Hay and Helen Gardener with House and Senate leaders as Speaker Gillette signs the resolution

The 19th Amendment (ratified in 1920) gave women the right to vote. Until this amendment became part of the U.S. Constitution, some states allowed women to vote and others did not.

To learn more about amendments to the Constitution, go to **www.lawforkids.org/ LawDocs/Amendments.cfm**.

Women's Suffrage

Wyoming became the first state to give women the right to vote in 1890. As a territory, it allowed women's **suffrage** beginning in 1869. By the time the 19th Amendment passed, many western states already allowed women to vote. The majority of states, however, had to change in order to follow the new amendment. A handful of states didn't ratify the 19th Amendment until 1950 or later! Mississippi, the last, ratified the amendment in 1984.

Comparing Powers of National and State Governments

There are two types of governmental powers: **exclusive** (held only by the federal or state government) and **concurrent** (shared between federal and state government).

Powers exclusive to the federal government include printing money, regulating trade between states and between countries, making treaties, conducting foreign policy, declaring war and providing armed forces, and establishing post offices.

Powers exclusive to individual state governments include issuing licenses, regulating trade within a state, holding elections, and establishing local governments.

Powers shared between the federal government and its states include collecting taxes, building roads, borrowing money, establishing courts, making and enforcing laws, establishing banks and corporations, spending money for the good of the general public, protecting public health and safety, and taking private property when necessary for public purposes (with proper compensation).

Understanding the Levels of Government

This target will help you understand the levels of government.

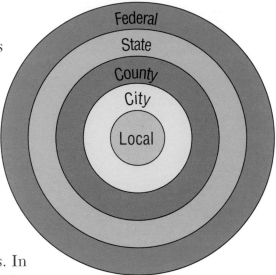

On the outside of the target is the federal government. The United States president and vice president, United States **legislators**, and members of the Supreme Court all belong to this level of government.

The second level of the target is state government. In what state do you live? We will learn more about the key players at this level in chapter 2.

The third level is **county** government. Most states have counties. In what county do you live? We will meet the county government officials who protect and serve you in chapter 3.

The fourth level is city government. In what city, town, or village do you live? The individuals who represent you locally reside in this ring of the target. We will learn more about them in chapter 4.

The center of the government is your local community. This could be your neighborhood, housing development, or block. It could also be your school!

The PBS Kids Democracy Project

www.pbs.org/democracy/ kids/mygovt/index.html

How does government affect everyday lives? Visit a virtual town and click on everyday objects and buildings to learn about the government's role.

Chapter 2

State Government

Washington, D.C., is the capital of the United States. Elected officials make and enforce federal laws there.

Each state has a capital city too. Laws and regulations on the state level are made and enforced from each state's capital. The capitol building is sometimes called the **statehouse**.

The U.S. Constitution *gives* states local power and *limits* the power each state has.

The capital city of Iowa—Des Moines

Capital vs. Capitol

The *capital* is the city that serves as the center of government. Washington, D.C., is the capital of the United States. It is the nation's headquarters. Your home state has a capital too. It is where your state **senators** and **representatives** meet to do business on a state level. The building in which legislators meet is called the *capitol*. U.S. senators and representatives meet in the nation's Capitol Building. Your state legislators meet in a capitol building in your state's capital.

Iowa's capitol building

Similar in Structure

State government is similar to federal government in structure. There is an executive branch, a legislative branch, and a judicial branch for each state. The executive branch enforces and executes the laws. The legislative branch makes the laws. The judicial branch interprets the laws. The number of elected officials and employed state workers in each branch varies from state to state. Often, these numbers depend on the size and population of the state.

Each state (and some of the nation's territories) has its own constitution. Some constitutions are short—Vermont's constitution barely tops 8,000 words, which is about the length of this book. And others are very long—Alabama's constitution is over 200,000 words!

When a state's constitution and the U.S. Constitution both cover an issue, the U.S. Constitution is more powerful. However, state constitutions can establish rules and guidelines for the state that are not covered in the U.S. Constitution. Like the U.S. Constitution, state constitutions can be amended or changed. To make changes to the state constitution, a **constitutional convention** must be held.

View Your State Constitution

What's included in your state constitution? You can view it at **www.prairienet.org/~scruffy/f.htm**.

The Governor: Head of State

Just as the president heads the federal government, a governor heads a state's government.

In the early days of America, governors of colonies were primarily **figureheads**. They were appointed by the king to represent the king's interest. The people of the colonies did not always trust their governors. The governors did not usually have the citizens' interests in mind.

After the creation of the U.S. Constitution, state legislatures appointed governors (in all but two states, where they were elected). Each governor served a one-year **term** and had limited powers.

Eventually, states created their own constitutions and gave more power to the executive branch—the governor. People learned that they could trust their governors to run the state with the citizens' interests in mind.

Today, all states elect their governors by popular vote. Most states have minimum requirements for **gubernatorial** candidates. These often include a minimum age and a length of residency. Only two states—Kansas and Ohio—have no requirements for gubernatorial candidates.

In most states, the governor holds office for a four-year term. (Vermont governors hold two-year terms.) Some states limit how many terms an individual can occupy the governor's chair.

While governors are the "heads of state" and are most closely aligned with the state's executive branch of government, their actual duties overlap all three branches of state government.

New York gubernatorial candidates, 2002

The Governor as Executive

As each state's executive, governors submit the state budget to the state legislature each year and prioritize state spending. They also oversee many governmental agencies and appoint individuals to some government positions.

They have certain military powers. Governors are the commanders-in-chief of the National Guard in their state.

Governors can declare natural disaster areas within their states. The states can then apply for federal disaster aid.

Virginia Governor Mark Warner greets members of the Virginia National Guard.

The Governor as Legislator

Governors represent the people of their state. They can propose legislation, usually during the State of the State address. This is the annual report given by governors to the legislature. In this address, governors outline state priorities.

Governors can also meet with legislators throughout their term to influence new laws. They can also request that the citizens of a state contact their local legislators to influence new laws and regulations.

In most states, governors have the authority to override, or **veto**, legislation.

The Governor as a Judicial Authority

Governors can also serve in a judicial role. They have this power through **executive clemency rules**. They can lessen sentences of convicted felons or overturn sentences altogether. They can pardon criminals and set them free. In states with **capital punishment** laws, a criminal scheduled for execution appeals to the governor to spare his or her life.

First Ladies or Gentlemen

The spouse of the governor is the state's first lady or first gentleman. She or he often plays an important role in the state. Like the spouse of the president, the spouse of a governor often adopts a special cause while his or her husband or wife is in office. Some common causes are literacy, early learning, health care, and the arts.

Oklahoma first lady and former teacher Kim Henry announces a major financial gift that will support early childhood education. Her husband, Governor Brad Henry, looks on.

Spotlight: Governors in the News

Nellie Taylor Ross

Wyoming's Nellie Taylor Ross became the first female governor in 1925. Her husband, William, was Wyoming's governor until 1924 when he died in office. The acting governor called for a **special election**. The Democratic Party nominated Nellie for the office. At first, she declined the nomination. Then she decided to run for governor. She won easily. Sixteen days later, Miriam A. Ferguson became governor of Texas. She, too, followed in her husband's footsteps, becoming governor after his second-term impeachment.

L. Douglas Wilder from Virginia became the first African American governor in 1989, more than 60 years after the country's first female governor was elected. Governor Wilder was first elected to the state **senate** in 1969. He served in that role until 1985. He was then elected lieutenant governor.

L. Douglas Wilder

Not all governors reach the statehouse through traditional election routes. On November 17, 2003, Arnold Schwarzenegger became the governor of California. The state ran a special recall election to determine whether to remove then-governor Gray Davis. Prior to his inauguration, Schwarzenegger was best known for his bodybuilding and movie roles.

Pathway to the White House

The chart below shows governors who have gone on to the White House as president.

Name	State	Years as Governor	Years as President
Thomas Jefferson	Virginia	1779–1781	1801–1809
James Monroe	Virginia	1799–1802	1817–1825
Martin Van Buren	New York	1828–1829	1837–1841
John Tyler	Virginia	1825–1827	1841–1845
James K. Polk	Tennessee	1839–1841	1845–1849
Andrew Johnson	Tennessee	1853–1857	1865–1869
Rutherford B. Hayes	Ohio	1867–1871; 1875–1877	1877–1881
Grover Cleveland	New York	1882–1884	1885–1889
William McKinley	Ohio	1892–1896	1897–1901
Theodore Roosevelt	New York	1898–1900	1901–1909
Woodrow Wilson	New Jersey	1911–1912	1913–1921
Calvin Coolidge	Massachusetts	1918–1920	1923–1929
Franklin D. Roosevelt	New York	1929–1933	1933–1945
Jimmy Carter	Georgia	1971–1975	1977–1981
Ronald Reagan	California	1967–1975	1981–1989
William J. Clinton	Arkansas	1979–1981; 1983–1992	1993–2001
George W. Bush	Texas	1994–2000	2001–

Other State Leaders

Lieutenant governors are second in command at the state level. Lieutenant governors are to governors as vice presidents are to presidents.

The primary responsibility of the lieutenant governor is to fill the position of governor if the governor is unable to complete his or her term.

Lieutenant governors may be granted authority over certain areas of state government. This is often based on their background. A lieutenant governor who was once a teacher may choose to work closely with the state's department of education, for example.

Lieutenant governors can be elected several ways. Sometimes the governor and lieutenant governor run together on one ticket. They are elected as a team and are usually from the same party.

Sometimes the governor and lieutenant governor run independently. Then it is possible that the two top state leaders will be from different parties.

Lieutenant governor candidate Kerry Healey waves to the crowd at a reception for her and her running mate, Mitt Romney. The pair won the election and became the leaders of Massachusetts' state government.

The Attorney General

The primary legal advisors in each state are the attorney generals. They have important legal duties, including representing the state in court. The attorney general interprets state law for state officials.

The attorney general is elected in all but seven states, where the governor appoints someone to the job.

The Secretary of State

Secretaries of state are responsible for all state documents and records. They (through their staff) issue business licenses and approve applications for the creation of corporations. They also serve as their state's election officers. They follow election law, prepare and distribute ballots, tally and report election results, and certify the election.

The secretary of state is elected in most states. Hawaii and Alaska do not have a secretary of state.

State Treasurer or Comptroller

The state treasurers or comptrollers are responsible for states' money. They collect it, invest it, and pay contractors and state employees. The treasurers oversee spending by state departments and collect taxes from state residents. The state comptroller is an elected position.

A Different Kind of Secretary of State

The title "secretary of state" is used in both federal and state governments, but the positions are not the same. States have secretaries of state to perform the functions outlined in this chapter. The federal government also has a secretary of state. He or she is part of the executive branch of government and reports to the president of the United States. The job responsibilities are quite different. The secretary of state on the federal level works closely with other countries and governments, representing the United States to foreign countries and the United Nations.

State Legislature

The powers and size of each state's legislature are determined by the state's constitution. Elected officials are called *legislators*.

In most states, the state legislature is structured like the federal legislative branch. This two-chambered system is known as a **bicameral** legislature. Nebraska is the only state with one chamber, known as a **unicameral** legislature.

Illinois Supreme Court Justice Charles E. Freeman (left) swears in Senator Emil Jones, Jr. (right) as the new Illinois Senate president.

The upper house is called the *senate*. The elected officials are called *state senators*. Senators represent a specific area of the state. The **president of the senate** is the senator who holds the most power and is a member of the majority party in the upper house.

Depending on the state, the lower house may be called the ***house of representatives*** or the ***house of delegates***. The elected officials are called *state representatives* or ***delegates***. Usually, there are more lower house members than upper house members. Each lower house member represents a smaller portion of the state than a senator does. The **speaker** is a representative or delegate who holds the most power and is a member of the majority party in the lower house.

Both houses of the state legislature are called the ***general assembly***.

The general assembly has two important responsibilities. It must monitor the health, safety, and welfare of the state. The state legislature also controls the state's money by passing the state's budget each year.

Legislators have the power to introduce and pass legislation that is important to the people they represent. This legislation must go through an approval process to become law.

Spending State Money

States spend the majority of their money on programs to help their residents. Some of the key spending areas are education, transportation, public health and welfare, environmental conservation, and law enforcement and correction.

The largest part of a state's budget impacts students (and their teachers) directly. About one-third of each state's money is spent on education. Some of the money for education comes from local government. Some education programs are federally funded. A portion of a state's education fund is used to operate state colleges and universities.

Each state is responsible for the roads within its borders. The state constructs new roads and maintains old roads. About ten percent of a state's budget is spent on its transportation system. In a few years, many of you may be applying for a driver's license. You will go to an office of your state's department of transportation to apply for your permit and to take your test.

Per Pupil Spending Statistics

In 2001, the state that spent the least was Utah ($4,579 per student). The state that spent the most was New Jersey ($9,362 per student). How much does your state spend on average for its students? Go to **www.stateline.org/ stateline/?pa=fact&sa=showFact&id =241395** to find out.

Each state is responsible for the health and welfare of its residents. About one-third of a state's budget is needed for this purpose. The state gives welfare benefits to those in need. Money is used to operate state-owned hospitals. Each state is concerned with medical issues, such as child health care and nursing homes.

As the United States grows, it is important that natural areas be protected for future generations to enjoy. States are partially responsible for conserving land.

Who Receives Welfare?

In 2000, more than one million people received welfare benefits in California. In the less-populated Wyoming, about one thousand individuals received benefits. How many individuals were in need of public assistance in your state? Click here to find out: **www.stateline.org/stateline/?pa =fact&sa=showFact&id=121**

State-Owned Lands and Parks

There are 93 state parks in Wisconsin, and more than 14 million people visit them each year. There are more than 50 state recreation areas in Hawaii. Alaska has 41 state-maintained trails in its state for a variety of recreational purposes. And the tiny state of Rhode Island has 17 state parks and 10 state beaches!

To learn more about parks in your state, including those that are state-owned, visit **www.parkmaps.com/US_Map _State_Selection.htm**.

Silver Falls State Park, Oregon

Monahans Sandhills State Park, Monahans, Texas

There are state parks for residents to enjoy. States regulate hunting and fishing. They also regulate pollution emissions and oversee the clean up of contaminated areas.

Texas created the first state police operation, the Texas Rangers, in 1835. Today, all 50 states have state police systems. The state police help with law enforcement. They maintain fingerprint databases. They operate criminal laboratories. And they hold prisoners, including juveniles, for the state.

Learning More About Your State Government

To learn more about your state government, visit **www.statelocalgov.net/index.cfm**.

Chapter 3

County Government

The United States has 50 states, and all of these states have smaller forms of government. Most states call these smaller areas *counties*. Counties are political subdivisions of states.

There are more than 3,000 counties in the United States! Delaware has the fewest number of counties—three. Texas has the most counties—254!

Not all states call these subdivisions *counties*. Louisiana has parishes and Alaska has boroughs.

Most counties contain several larger cities or towns. But some counties are made up of only one city. San Francisco and Denver are cities. They are also counties.

Colorado Counties

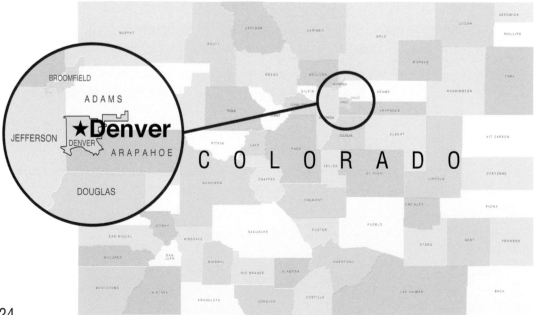

Protecting Its Residents

Counties must follow the rules of the state. Residents depend on county officials and departments to protect them. They rely on counties to take care of their roads.

County officials protect residents' rights. They enforce laws, maintain order, and hold county prisoners.

Counties collect taxes. They store marriage and birth certificates. They record property deeds. Some counties provide health services and recreation. And some counties provide fire protection and library services.

Counties may be involved with water, sewer, and electrical services. They may maintain a county airport. Some schools are managed on a county level. Rural county government may be involved with agriculture.

Forms of County Government

Not all county governments are organized the same. The most common type of county government is a **commission**. It is a **board** of department heads, such as the **sheriff** or chief engineer, who enforce the laws. Most board members are elected officials. They usually serve four-year terms.

Another form of county government is a **council**. Representatives of the county's villages and towns select managers to oversee departments within the county.

Some county governments model the federal government and have three branches: executive, legislative, and judicial.

Let's meet some of the key players in county government.

Key County Officials

Most county officials are elected by popular vote.

County residents usually elect their county sheriffs for four-year terms. Sheriffs supervise a workforce of patrol officers, manage the county jail, serve legal papers, and may handle county emergency (9-1-1) calls. Sheriffs' departments are involved in educating young residents about the dangers of drugs and protecting them while in school. Sheriffs' departments focus on rural areas within the counties.

An Interview with County Sheriff Tom Lorey

Sheriff Tom Lorey has led the sheriff's department of a 550-square-mile county of 58,000 people for the past eight years. In 2003 alone, his department received almost 48,000 calls through the 9-1-1 emergency system. During his time in office, he has witnessed firsthand the challenges faced by young people in his community. And he has watched his department's role change to meet those challenges.

★ *How has your department changed during the eight years you have sat in the sheriff's seat?*

My department has grown to 109 full-time employees. There are 39 road patrol personnel. The majority of my full-time employees work in corrections. And we have three K-9s (dogs), named Blitz, Kane, and Bosco. Initially, the dogs focused on illegal drug detection. Since September 11, [2001] one of our dogs specializes in explosives.

★ *How would you describe the region that you and your officers patrol?*

I work for a county that is mostly rural. It is our responsibility to protect the people that live outside the city limits. And our population is shifting from the city to the country, so our responsibilities have increased.

★ *What are some of the greatest challenges facing young people in your area?*

It has always been difficult for some teens to go through that final growth process into adulthood. It is a confusing time. And sometimes teens make bad decisions.

Living in a rural community has its advantages, however. We don't have the same amount of peer pressure and neighborhood gangs. In many ways, it is a bit simpler way of life.

Unfortunately, our rural community is an area that has one of the highest rates of unemployment. This sad statistic impacts families, and children don't often receive the parenting they need or deserve because of family stress.

Some of our inmates have witnessed domestic violence in their homes (or have been involved directly with the violence). Society recognizes this as a major problem. In the past, our goal was to stop the fighting in the household. Today, social agencies become involved immediately and arrests are often made.

★ *Who is your typical inmate?*

The majority of "residents" in our county jail are under the age of 19. Our prison population averages 120, and the maximum we can hold is 167. In our state, youth are considered adults at the age of 16, and that is the minimum age that we can accommodate here at our facility.

★ *What does the county do to help these young offenders take the right path?*

We have a progressive inmate education program. The average time spent here in our facility is four months. The longest an inmate can stay in the county jail is one year. During an inmate's incarceration, we work hard to see that the majority of residents pass the General Educational Development (GED) test. It opens up a door of opportunity for them.

★ *As a young adult growing up, what doors of opportunity were opened for you?*

I had several mentors growing up. Believe it or not, one of them was my assistant principal. I came to know him personally due to juvenile mischief! He spent time with me (or I spent time with him!) every day. He showed me an environment of learning, and I came to respect him well.

★ *How has the school environment changed since you were there?*

The General Education Development (GED) Test

The GED is a test distributed by the department of education in each state. By passing the GED, a person who has not graduated from high school can earn a high school equivalency diploma. This allows them to apply for college admission or to obtain employment that requires a high school diploma. The GED is made up of five tests: Language Arts, Reading, Social Studies, Science, and Math. The tests measure understanding at the average skill level of a high school senior. On average, one out of every seven people to earn a high school diploma each year does so by passing the GED. Visit **www.gedtest.org** for more information.

Since the Columbine shootings [in Littleton, Colorado, on April 20, 1999], we changed the way we look at schools. We practice emergency events in the school buildings. We coordinate our efforts with the **school**

districts. We educate the educators, too, sharing trouble signs with them. Today, schools are much safer.

★ *What is the D.A.R.E. program and what is your involvement?*

D.A.R.E stands for Drug Abuse Resistance Education. The effort started in Los Angeles in 1983. We have a D.A.R.E. officer in each of our middle schools. He works closely with sixth graders to help them understand the dangers of drugs and what they can do to say "no." We are part of our community and want the students to see us as a positive influence in their lives.

★ *Were there other experiences as a student that shaped your career choice?*

My entire family was involved with the local volunteer fire department. I wanted to follow in their footsteps. I became a young member of the volunteer fire department. I learned that I liked helping other people.

★ *How do you prepare for new challenges on your job?*

Like the students reading this, I learn every day. There is no minimum number of hours of required instruction for my department. We are learning constantly through in-service programs and drills.

★ *For students interested in a law enforcement career, what would you recommend?*

Do well in school. Explore law enforcement/security programs at your vocational-technical school. Look into college programs too. And find yourself a mentor to guide you. (He or she may be sitting in your principal's office right now!)

County auditors are the money managers. They take in the county's money and pay the county's bills. Auditors may also establish property taxes and distribute tax dollars to state institutions.

One way the county may raise money is through property taxes. **County assessors** determine the monetary value of property by performing an **assessment**. Taxes are based on this assessment. Property taxes are used to pay for schools, libraries, and other services.

The **county surveyor** sets boundary lines by surveying. Surveyors measure angles and distances on the ground with special instruments. They then accurately plot the results on a map. County surveyors determine where new roads or waterlines may go. They also make adjustments to boundary lines when the land changes. Floods, earthquakes, and landslides can move boundary lines.

County clerks are responsible for registering and recording land ownership changes in the county. They also records births, deaths, marriages, and divorces. Individuals researching their family history often spend time in the county clerks' offices examining records. County clerks may also issue hunting and fishing licenses. The county clerk is part of the county's legal system.

A key member of the county's legal system is the **district attorney**. Another name for district attorney is ***prosecutor***. Prosecutors are the attorneys for the counties. District attorneys investigate crimes. They determine when an individual should be charged. And district attorneys try cases in court too. The district attorney has a staff of support people and other attorneys to assist in this big job. Helping crime victims is another important part of this position.

An Interview with District Attorney Louise K. Sira

At the age of 36, Louise K. Sira is one of the youngest elected officials to hold the position of district attorney. She serves a population of about 55,000 people. Her decisions have lifelong effects on the people involved directly in cases, their families, and the greater community she serves. In addition to working for her district, she is also the mother of two small boys and a community leader.

★ *When you graduated from law school in 1993, did you envision yourself in the role of district attorney?*

Yes, I did! In eighth grade I wrote a story about my future. I wanted to be a criminal lawyer who served on the prosecution side of the law. I was given a gift early in life. I knew what I wanted to be when I grew up. I never struggled with what classes to take or what college to attend.

★ *What factors influenced your career decision at such an early age?*

I loved watching television shows and reading books about law. I was an avid reader, and I digested Nancy Drew and Hardy Boys books. I played "private investigator" when I was a child. And one year I even dressed up as a detective for Halloween! It was one of my favorite costumes.

★ *Did you have a mentor or teacher who helped guide your career?*

When I was in high school, I had an English teacher for two years who pushed me in a positive direction. He challenged me to stretch my writing skills. He reminded me of the importance of good grammar and expressing yourself clearly so others know what you are saying.

But perhaps my real mentor was my mom. She was a kindergarten teacher in the city school district. She believed in education. She raised us to be independent thinkers. And she also offered us exposure to diverse cultures and experiences.

★ *How did you become a district attorney?*

After graduating from college and law school, I sent my resume to every district attorney's office from Maine to Florida. I was determined. Several district offices granted me interviews. I accepted a position as an assistant district attorney in Fulton County (New York). In a small office such as this one, you are thrown right into town court. My first year out of law school, I wrote search warrants, conducted drug raids, worked on appeals, and heard traffic court cases.

★ *What was your career path to your current position?*

I served as an assistant district attorney for three years. I was then promoted to first assistant district attorney. I worked at this level for six years, when I was appointed district attorney. District attorneys are not usually appointed. They are elected. We had a special situation in our office. Our current district attorney was elected as judge. Someone had to jump in and fill her shoes. And that was me! In the next election, the voters did elect me as their district attorney.

★ *How did school prepare you for the election process?*

Like young students today, I studied about the election process. And I was a registered voter. But neither prepared me as a candidate. It was new for me. It was scary,

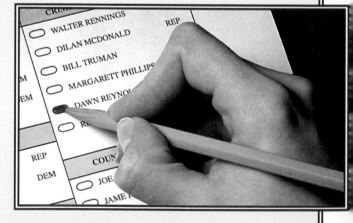

yet exciting. I enjoyed the many opportunities to meet the public and discuss issues in the criminal justice system.

I had always focused on my job. Now I had to focus on me. I was not used to doing that. Many of the local voters did not know me. I grew up about two hours away from my district. The voters did not know me personally, so I had to educate them. I needed to tell them who I was. I shared with them my experiences of working for them for the past several years. I told them about the major cases I worked on for them. And most importantly, I had to tell them my name (and they had to remember it!).

★ *What are your primary responsibilities as district attorney?*

As the chief law enforcement officer in the county, I prosecute cases when law enforcement agencies have made arrests. I investigate charges through a grand jury process. And I litigate, or go to trial on, cases that cannot be settled.

But perhaps my most important responsibility is that I am a public officer. I provide community services. I visit schools. I participate in the D.A.R.E. program, promote literacy, coach mock trial teams, participate in civic organizations, sit on boards of directors, and support the victim's advocacy program for the county.

★ *What is the greatest challenge in your job?*

My greatest challenge is balancing the number and variety of situations that come into my office each and every day.

★ *How do you spend a typical day?*

I go to court; conduct hearings; write motions, briefs, and memorandums of law; prepare for trial; follow up with witness interviews, etc. I also attend meetings with other law enforcement professionals. I go to press announcements. I attend community meetings. I spend time in the schools. I supervise a staff of ten people.

I spend much of my day listening and reviewing letters, papers, police reports, and statements. Sometimes listening can lead to big breaks. A conversation with someone filing a complaint about dog waste led to us solving a missing person/fraud case. What if I had not been listening to what was being said?

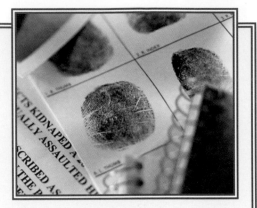

★ *How has crime changed over the ten years you have worked in the district attorney's office?*

The biggest change I have witnessed is drug crimes. Ten years ago, we prosecuted mostly marijuana and cocaine crimes. Today, these crimes involve LSD, heroin, methamphetamine, and ecstasy. The drugs and the way they are ingested are more and more deadly. Sadly, the ages of the users and dealers have become younger.

★ *What social factors impact your work?*

Children have been and will always be my top priority. But factors that impact how children are cared for include unemployment, drug and alcohol abuse, and the age of the parents. Young parents have fewer life experiences to call upon to help them guide their children's lives.

★ *As a middle school student, what did you learn that prepared you for the job you hold today?*

I liked middle school. I enjoyed my English, social studies, and research and library classes. Learning to use reference materials and prepare research papers with footnotes has helped me greatly in my job today. And, of course, reading, reading, reading!

> ★ *For the young student thinking of a career in law, what would you recommend?*
>
> First, make schoolwork your priority. Develop good study habits. Don't procrastinate! If you have an assignment, do it. It is human nature to put it off until later, but fight that urge. Try to work ahead of schedule. Discipline yourself and don't rely on others. Become self-motivated. And learn to manage your workload. In college and law school, you must juggle many assignments at one time.

Sometimes deaths occur that need to be investigated. The **county coroner** tries to determine the cause of death. It may be from an accident. It may be from an unknown illness. If a death occured as a result of violence, the county coroner may work with the district attorney.

Know Your County

Venture on an online exploration to discover information about the county in which you live. Learn its county seat, elected officials, population changes, square miles served, and types of businesses within the county.

Go to **www.naco.org/Template.cfm? Section=Data_and_Demographics&Template =/cffiles/counties/city_srch.cfm**.

Chapter 4

Community Government

M ost people live in cities, towns, or villages. Cities are areas of greater size, population, or importance than towns or villages. They all have governing systems to protect and serve their residents.

The municipality is one kind of city government. Each city, town, or village must be approved by the state. Each has a **charter** that outlines its responsibilities. The charter allows the area to govern itself. It describes the job duties of the city, town, or village leaders.

Cities, towns, and villages have many of the same responsibilities as counties. They must provide services to protect their residents. They provide health and education services. They offer programs for those with special needs.

Head of the City

Mayors are the heads of most cities. The people living in the city elect them. They usually serve a two- or four-year term. They are responsible for their residents, similar to governors' responsibility to state residents. The mayor usually reports to the **city council**.

The city council helps the mayor govern the city. Most cities have city councils. Council members are elected. They are sometimes called **aldermen**. They meet regularly to discuss city issues.

Miami Mayor Joe Carollo holds a news conference.

Council members representing the entire city are called *council members* **at-large**. Council members can also represent a section of the city known as a **ward**.

City councils can pass **ordinances**. These are rules and regulations that the council thinks will make the city a better place to live. Sometimes, mayors can override, or veto, city ordinances.

City councils can decide how land will be used by creating **zones** within their city for specific purposes. The council can zone an area industrial (for factories) or agricultural (for farming). It can determine where single-family homes can be and where multiple-family dwellings (like apartments) can be located.

Mayors may prepare city-spending plans. The council has the power to accept the budget or disapprove it.

Sometimes two cities **consolidate**, or merge. Then the two can share resources. Consolidation helps small communities save money. Often, some residents are not in favor of consolidation. They are afraid that the heritage of the individual cities or towns will be lost.

Some cities have **city managers**. They are professional managers with education and experience in management. Cities with **city manager-council** governments have mayors too. But the mayor is usually elected by the city council. City managers prepare the budget. They oversee the city departments and may appoint people to head them.

Passion Lands Mayor in Trouble with Police

Bill Pollak loves his city of Johnstown in upstate New York. When he was mayor, he was so passionate about its beauty that it almost put him in jail. Twice.

Pollak was a stickler when it came to trash. He strolled around his neighborhood picking up blowing papers and discarded fast-food wrappers. He encouraged his neighbors to plant trees. And he delivered trash intended for garbage collection—but placed on the curbside too late (or much too early)—back to its originator for safekeeping. (Some of these residents did not appreciate the mayor coming onto their properties and called the police.)

Pollak was a believer in community action. As a former teacher of government and civics in the high school, he tried to set an example for his students.

Other City Positions

Most cities have a **chief of police** who manages the police force. The police department maintains law and order within the city.

Most cities have paid fire departments. The head of the fire department is called the **fire chief**.

Cities may have a **superintendent** who is responsible for the water department or a plant manager who cares for the wastewater treatment facility. A dog warden may catch unleashed dogs. A tax collector receives tax money from residents. A city historian records events and collects newspaper clippings. It takes many people to run a city.

Most population centers have libraries. The head of the library is called the *director*. Libraries receive funding from several sources and service their direct community and outlying areas too. Many libraries are at risk for closing. There is not enough money in city budgets to keep the doors open.

A Special Community: Schools

Every United States resident is guaranteed a free public education. In order to provide this education, there are more than 15,000 school districts. Each was established by the state in which it is located. The day-to-day operation of the schools, however, is run at a local level.

School districts can be large or small, depending on where they are located. A school district may be one school or many schools. Some districts have different buildings for different age groups. Other school districts have all students in one building.

Most money for schools comes from local property taxes. Schools that are located in poorer areas may not receive as much money from property owners as those located in more affluent neighborhoods.

School districts also receive federal and state money. Both the federal and state governments have formulas and guidelines to determine the amount given to a school district.

Eddie Miller, school superintendent of the Norphlet School District (left) and Rodney Barnette, school superintendent of the Union School District (right) answer questions during an Arkansas Department of Education board meeting.

School boards guide most school efforts. Sometimes the residents who live in the area that the school serves elect school board members. The mayor may appoint school board members.

The school board may determine what students will study and what books students will use. They may decide if students will have a dress code or vending machines in the cafeteria. The school board (or the mayor) also selects the school superintendent. He or she is responsible for what happens in each school.

Knowing Your Local Government: A Hands-On Approach

Who is your mayor? Who are your legislators? What decisions is your school board making that affect you? Learning about government begins in your own backyard. Discover more about your local government by reading your local paper. Bring articles in to your classroom to share with your teacher and classmates. Attend a school board meeting. Write your own article on what you learned. Be an informed citizen. Let your voice be heard.

EDMOND H. TAVEIRNE
MIDDLE SCHOOL
LEARNING CENTER
34699 N. Highway 12
Ingleside, IL 60041

THE WORLD

Internet Connections
and Related Readings
for State and Local Government

bensguide.gpo.gov

Enter Ben's Guide to U.S. Government for Kids and explore the branches of government and other interesting topics that relate to the U.S. government.

www.kids.gov/k_states.htm

Find a link to your state's kid-friendly Web site at this location.

www.wordiq.com/definition/County_statistics_of_the_United_States

This Web page provides links to each state's smallest and largest counties. Click on the county name for more information.

www.statelocalgov.net/

A complete guide to state and local government, featuring links to each state's Web site and detailed information about their governments.

★　★　★　★　★　★　★

The Voice of the People: American Democracy in Action by Betsy Maestro. Explains how our leaders, from local mayors to presidents and Supreme Court justices, go about earning their jobs, and just what their jobs are. William Morrow, 1998. [RL 4 IL 1–5] (5718501 PB)

What Are My Rights? 95 Questions and Answers About Teens and the Law by Thomas A. Jacobs, J.D. A Superior Court judge encourages teens to know their rights and do the right thing. Covers teen rights at home, school, work, individually, and within the legal system. Includes charts, adoption request information, a glossary, and index. Free Spirit, 1997. [RL 7 IL 7–12] (5597901 PB)

The letters *RL* in the brackets indicate the reading level of the book listed. *IL* indicates the approximate interest level. Perfection Learning's catalog numbers are included for your ordering convenience. *PB* indicates paperback.

Glossary

aldermen (AWL dur men) members of a city council

assessment (uh SES muhnt) determination of the monetary value of a property

at-large (*at large*) representing an entire area

bicameral (beye CAM ruhl) having two legislative houses

board (*board*) group of people that serves as a governing body

borough (BUR oh) division of Alaska similar to a county in most other states

capital punishment (KAP i tul PUN ish muhnt) death as a penalty for committing a crime

charter (CHAR tur) document that outlines a city's powers and responsibilities and describes the duties of its leaders

chief of police (cheef *of* puh LEES) head of a police department

city council (*city* KOWN suhl) group of elected members who help the mayor govern the city

city manager (*city* MAN uh jur) professional who prepares the budget for and oversees departments of a city

city manager-council (*city* MAN uh jur KOWN suhl) type of government in which the city manager and city council work together. The city manager is appointed by the council, which is made up of elected officials.

commission (kuh MISH shuhn) group of elected officials that governs a county

concurrent (kuhn KUR uhnt) powers shared between federal and state government

consolidate (kuhn SOL uh dayt) to merge so as to share resources

constitutional convention (kon stuh TOO shuhn uhl kuhn VEN shuhn) meeting of a state's legislature for the purpose of discussing and voting on proposed amendments to that state's constitution

council (KOWN suhl) group of representatives who select managers to oversee county departments

county (KOWN tee) political subdivision of a state

county assessor (KOWN tee uh SES ur) individual who assesses property value in a county

county auditor (KOWN tee AW duh tur) individual in charge of managing a county's money, paying its bills, establishing property taxes, and distributing tax money

county clerk (KOWN tee *clerk*) individual responsible for land, birth, death, marriage, and divorce records as well as other licenses in a county

county coroner (KOWN tee KOR uh nur) individual in charge of investigating deaths that may not be due to natural causes

county surveyor (KOWN tee sur VEY ur) individual responsible for measuring, calculating distances, and plotting results on a map so as to plan for new roads or waterlines in a county

delegate (DEL uh guht) elected official who serves in the house of delegates (see separate glossary entry)

district attorney (DIS trikt uh TURN ee) county attorney who investigates crimes, brings charges against individuals, and tries cases in court; also called a *prosecutor* (see separate glossary entry)

exclusive (eks KLOO siv) powers held only by the federal or state government

executive clemency rules (ig ZEK you tiv KLEM en see roolz) power by which a governor can lessen, overturn, and pardon sentences of convicted criminals

federalism (FED uh ruhl ism) type of government in which power is shared between the federal government and its states

figurehead (FIG yur hed) leader in name only

fire chief (feyer cheef) head of a fire department

general assembly (JEN uh ruhl uh SEM blee) both houses of a state's legislative body

gubernatorial (goo ber nuh TOR ee uhl) of or relating to a governor

house of delegates (*house of* DEL uh guhts) legislative body of a state's government

house of representatives (*house of* rep ruh ZEN tuh tivs) legislative body of a state's government

legislator (LEJ uhs lay tur) term for an elected official who serves in a state's legislature

mayor (may ur) elected official who heads a city government

ordinances (OR duh nuhn ses) rules and regulations for a city

parish (PAIR ish) division of Louisiana similar to a county in most other states

president of the senate (PREZ uh dent *of the* SEN uht) senator who has the most power in the upper house of a state's legislature and is a member of the majority party

prosecutor (PRAW suh kyou tur) county attorney who investigates crimes, brings charges against individuals, and tries cases in court; also called a *district attorney* (see separate glossary entry)

ratify (RAT i feye) to approve formally

representative (rep ruh ZEN tuh tiv) elected official who serves in the house of representatives (see separate glossary entry)

school district (skool DIS trikt) unit that governs a school or group of schools within a state

senate (SEN uht) one half of a state's bicameral (see separate glossary entry) legislature

senator (SEN uh tur) member of the senate

sheriff (SHAIR uhf) county official in charge of law enforcement and other legal actions

speaker (SPEEK ur) representative or delegate who has the most power in the lower house of a state's legislature and is a member of the majority party

special election (SPEH shuhl i LEK shuhn) election that takes place to fill a position that has suddenly become open

statehouse (STAYT *house*) building in which a state's legislature meets

suffrage (SUHF rij) relating to the right to vote in public elections

superintendent (soo pur in TEN duhnt) person in charge

term (*term*) length of time one person serves in office

unicameral (you ni KAM ruhl) having one house

veto (VEE toh) power or right to reject something

ward (*ward*) division of a city for governing purposes

zone (*zone*) area set aside for a specific purpose

Index